Swankyswigs ®

Mark and Sheila Moore

4880 Lower Valley Road, Atglen, PA 19310 USA

Published by Schiffer Publishing Ltd.
4880 Lower Valley Road
Atglen, PA 19310
Phone: (610) 593-1777; Fax: (610) 593-2002
E-mail: Info@schifferbooks.com
Please visit our web site catalog at **www.schifferbooks.com**
We are always looking for people to write books on new and related subjects.
If you have an idea for a book please contact us at the above address.

This book may be purchased from the publisher.
Include $3.95 for shipping.
Please try your bookstore first.
You may write for a free catalog.

In Europe, Schiffer books are distributed by
Bushwood Books
6 Marksbury Ave.
Kew Gardens
Surrey TW9 4JF England
Phone: 44 (0) 20 8392-8585; Fax: 44 (0) 20 8392-9876
E-mail: Bushwd@aol.com
Free postage in the U.K., Europe; air mail at cost.

Mark and Sheila Moore may be reached at:
P.O. Box F
Rimersburg, PA 16248
Email: swankyswigman@hotmail.com
Website: http://www.koolpages.com/swankyswigs

Copyright © 2003 by Mark and Sheila Moore
Library of Congress Card Number: 2003101742

Cover and layout designed by Bruce Waters
Type set in Korinna BT

ISBN: 0-7643-1844-6
Printed in China

Acknowledgments

I would like to thank all those who have helped with photos or information used in this book.

There are a lot of nice collections out there and you will meet a few of the collectors in this book. Lane Howell, Joyce Jackson, Rachel Rasminsky, Nancy Garson, and Carol Nelson have shared their collections to help make this book. They have provided many of the photos and their knowledge and we would like to thank them for their help.

I also would like to thank my wife Sheila, our children, Kristen and Lindsey, and grandchildren, Colton and Anna Marie, for putting up with me spending hours and hours at the computer trying to acquire the information on the history and pricing it took to make this Swankyswig book possible.

A Note about Values

The current values in this book should only be used as a guide. They are not intended to set prices. Prices are from market sales and auctions sales and can vary from location to location. The author assumes no responsibility for any losses that might be incurred as a result of consulting this guide.

Dedication

To my parents, Paul and Maxine Moore, and to the memory of my grandfather, Bruce Moore, who started my wife and I in collecting and selling over 23 years ago.

Contents

"Swankyswig"
The History of the Name

"Swankyswigs" have been associated with Kraft® since they were first introduced in 1933. The glasses, first known as tumblers, were an immediate sales success. Kraft® had been selling cheese spreads in glass containers for some time prior to this, but the decorated tumbler offered new marketing potentials. Company officials felt that a decorated reusable tumbler would make a highly desirable, built-in premium for cheese spread products, rewarding those who bought them with a nicely decorated drinking glass. The problem was to develop a name for the glasses that would be easy to say and remember, and would have a strong party connection.

It was decided not to describe the containers as "cocktail" glasses and after considerable testing and sampling, the name *Swankyswig* was approved by Kraft®. One of the greatest premium offers in merchandising history was underway.

The name can be found on boxes and ads as Swankyswig, Swankyswigs and Swanky Swig. But the first name Swankyswig was and still is the official name.

American and Canadian Issue
1933 Band

The Band set was the first in the series of Swankyswigs. They were hand painted, which gives them a variation of colored rings in different locations.

The first Swankyswig was the red and black Band glass and you can see from the photos that different varieties can be found on the placement of the bands.

The most common glass to find is the four bands with red and black colors and can be found in two sizes 3 3/8' and 4 3/4" glass. The 4 3/4" glass was a mayonnaise Swankyswig.

There are other colors that have been reported like 3 3/8" yellow and red banded and a 3 3/8" green and white banded glasses but we can't confirm these as Kraft Swankyswigs.

White-Blue-Blue-White, $5.00, Blue-Blue, $5.00

Two varieties of Red-Black, $5.00 each

Black-Red-Black-Red 4 3/4", $7.00; 3 3/8", $4.00

Other Band, 3 3/8"

Red-Blue-Blue-Red	$10.00
Red-Blue-Red	N/A
Red-Green-Red-Green	$25.00
Red-Yellow-Red-Yellow	$25.00
Green-White	$25.00

The lid and jar shown here were used by Kraft® in the early 1930s. Although not a Swankyswig lid, it advertises the 4-band Blue and White Swankyswig that was available beginning in 1933. The lid urges the buyer to try "7 varieties of Kraft® cheese spreads in Swankyswig drinking glasses." Today Swankyswig has been broken into two separate words "Swanky Swig." This lid sells from $30.00 and up.

Jar with lid, $30.00

Lid only, $25.00

1934 Diamonds

To date, only two of these glasses have been reported found, both in red. This glass is 3 1/2" high and may have come in 4 colors: Green, Red, Blue, and Black. They are rare and I have not seen any of these on the internet auctions or at the antique markets. This glass is from *Lane Howell's* collection.

3 1/2" Red, rare

1935 Lattice and Vine

Now this set is a real challenge. The prices have gone up pretty high. They are 3 1/2" high and came in 4 colors. The design is white lattice with flowers in one of the following colors: green, red, blue, or black. Blue and black have not been found in anyone's collection to date. These glasses are from *Lane Howell's* collection.

3 1/2" Red, $150.00+

3 1/2" Green, $150.00+

1935 Circle and Dot

This set of Swankyswigs came in red, green, black, and blue. There are two sizes of glasses 3 1/2" and 4 3/4". The taller ones are hard to find. The hardest ones to locate are green and black (to date only one has been found in green and none in black). Note: The width of the lid for the tall one is 2 3/8" and the small lid is 2 3/16". There is also a solid dot swank, it is rare and I have seen only one on an Internet auction.

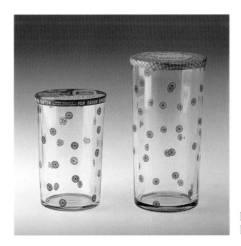

Blue, 3 1/2",$5.00;
Blue, 4 3/4", $12.00

Circle and Dot, 4 3/4"
          Green   rare
          Black   rare

Red, 3 1/2, $5.00; Red, 4 3/4", $12.00   Black, 3 1/2", $8.00; Green, 3 1/2", $8.00

1935 Star #1

The Star Swankyswigs came in red, green, black, blue, and yellow, and in two sizes: the 3 1/2" glass and the 4 3/4" glass. The 3 1/2" glasses are easy to find except in yellow. The yellow glass has been found in Canada. The 4 3/4" black and green glasses have not been found at the time of this printing although four orange glasses have been found.

This glass can also be found in a 4 7/8" cobalt blue glass.

Note: The Australian Star Swankyswig glasses are 3 3/8" high.

The orange star glass is from the *Lane Howell's* collection and the yellow star glass is from the *Rachel Rasminsky and Nancy Garson* collection.

Yellow Star, rare   Orange Star, rare   Cobalt 4 7/8", $45.00+

10

Red, 3 1/2", $5.00; Red, 4 3/4", $12.00

Blue, 3 1/2", $5.00; Blue, 4 3/4", $12.00

Black, 3 1/2", $8.00; with label, $40.00; Green, 3 1/2", $8.00

Star #1 Cookbook Ad

The ad from a 1936 Kraft® cook book shows the large glasses as a mayonnaise glass selling Ham-N-Aise.

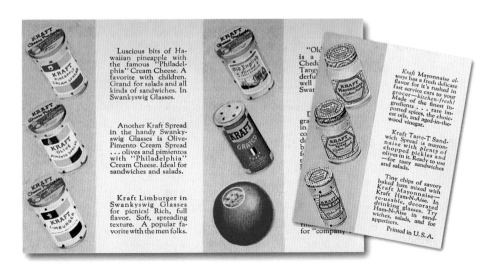

1936 Checkerboard

This glass came with white checkers and one of the following: red, green, or blue checkers. There are two sizes, the 3 1/2" glass and the 4 1/2" glass. The taller ones are rare and hard to find. They are the same shape as the Star glasses and, thanks to Carol Nelson, we now have a photo of the blue Swankyswig glass.

There is a look-alike glass that collectors are buying for their sets. It is 4 5/8" and is shaped like the 1970s Canadian Swankyswigs. They are selling for $15.00 and up.

There is also a checker Swankyswig that can be found in Canada. It is 3 1/8" high and the colors start with black at the top and one of the following colors: red, yellow, orange, or white. We haven't seen any of these for sale and don't know of anyone who has one. They are rare.

Red, 3 1/2", $15.00; Red, 4 5/8", $15.00

Blue, 3 1/2", $18.00; Green, 3 1/2", $18.00

4 9/16" checkerboard, rare

Checkerboard, 4 1/2"

Red	rare
Blue	rare
Green	rare

Checkerboard, 4 5/8"

Red	$15.00
Blue	$15.00
Green	$15.00

1936 Sailboat #1

This 4 5/8" glass seems to be found more in Canada than the United States. The 3 1/2" can be found in both places. There are 4 colors: red, yellow, orange, and blue. The taller ones are hard to find but the 3 1/2" glasses are even more difficult to locate. We have only seen the blue one for sale. I hope the one with the label shows everyone that this is a Swankyswig. We still can't confirm that the 4 5/8' glass is a Swankyswig.

There is also a look-alike glass that is 4 3/4" high, If you look at the photo it is the orange one next to the red one. Also watch out for the look-alike 3 1/2' glass, the top is 2 3/4" in diameter instead of 2 3/8" like most of the small Swankyswigs.

Blue, 3 1/2", $8.00

The orange one is a look-alike.

With label, $40.00+

Sailboat #1, 3 1/2"

Blue	$8.00
Red	rare
Green	rare
Orange	rare

Sailboat #1, 4 5/8"

Blue	$20.00
Red	$20.00
Green	$20.00
Orange	$20.00

1936 Sailboat #2

This has been an interesting set to put together. The 3 1/2" glass came in red, green, lime green, and blue. The 4 7/8" glass came in red, blue, black, and teal green. The lime green 3 1/2" glass is missing from a lot of collections, and no one else has reported the red one with two different size ships. The 4 7/8" glasses are not confirmed Swankyswigs. The black glass came out of a collection in Pennsylvania. It is a little different than the others. The birds and flags are smaller and the pattern is lower on the glass. I haven't seen a teal green or black 4 7/8" glass for sale on the Internet auctions or in antique markets.

Red, $18.00; Teal Green, rare; Blue, $18.00; and Black, rare

Dark Green, $18.00; Lime Green, rare

Regular Red Sailboat, $15.00; Small Red Sailboat, rare

Sailboat #2, 3 1/2"

Lime Green	rare
Dark Green	$18.00
Red	$15.00
Blue	$15.00

Sailboat #2, 4 7/8"

Red	$18.00
Blue	$18.00
Teal Green	rare
Black	rare

Blue Sailboat, $15.00

1937 Tulip #1

This is a set that takes some time to finish. They came in red, green, black, and blue, and in three sizes: 3 1/4", 3 1/2" and 4 5/8", with the taller ones being harder to find. The 4 5/8" black tulip is missing from most collections with only one reportedly found.

Green, 4 5/8", $30.00; 3 1/2", $5.00; 3 1/4", $18.00

Red, 4 5/8", $18.00; 3 1/2", $5.00; 3 1/4", $12.00

Blue, 4 5/8", $ 30.00; 3 1/2", $5.00; 3 1/4", $18.00

Black, 4 5/8", rare; 3 1/2", $5.00; 3 1/4", $18.00

1938 Tulip #2

This set is semi-rare. They came in only one size, 3 1/2", and four colors: red, green, black, and blue. They have molded rings around the top. They were made only for a short time and were sold exclusively on the west coast. I have seen more being sold on the Internet auction sites lately, so watch for them.

Red, $25.00; Blue, $25.00; Green, $25.00; Black, $25.00

1939 Carnival Ware

This set goes with many different décors. They came in one size, 3 1/2", and four colors: red, green, yellow, and blue. They were made for a short time to take advantage of Fiesta Ware, the popular dishes of the period. Watch out for fading or paint chips on this set.

Red, $8.00; Yellow, $8.00; Green, $8.00; Blue, $8.00

1939 Carnival Swankyswig Ad
This is a great ad showing the Carnival Ware glasses. It comes out of a 1939 Saturday Evening Post.

1939 ad, $40.00+

1941-46 Posy

There are four different flowers in the Posy Swankyswig set: Cornflower in light blue and dark blue, Jonquil in yellow, Tulips in red and Violet in blue. They came in three sizes: 3 1/4", 3 1/2", and 4 5/8" and will sell for more money in the spring than at any other time of year. Please note Kraft® spelled it as Posy (see ads).

Posy, 3 1/4"

Cornflower Light Blue	$7.00
Cornflower Dark Blue	$7.00
Jonquil	$7.00
Tulips	$7.00
Violets	$7.00

Posy, 3 1/2 "

Cornflower Light Blue	$6.00
Cornflower Dark Blue	$6.00
Jonquil	$6.00
Tulips	$6.00
Violets	$6.00

Posy, 4 5/8 "

Cornflower Light Blue	$20.00+
Cornflower Dark Blue	$20.00+
Jonquil	$20.00+
Tulips	$20.00+
Violets	$20.00+

1941 Posy Ad

This is a nice ad showing the posy glasses from 1941.

1941 ad, $15.00

1947 Cornflower #2

These Swankyswig glasses come in three sizes with 4 1/4" tall glasses being very hard to find. The 3 1/2" and 3 1/4" glasses are fairly common.

Label glass, $18.00

Cornflower #2, 3 1/4"

Red	$5.00
Light Blue	$5.00
Dark Blue	$5.00
Yellow	$5.00

Cornflower #2, 3 1/2"

Red	$5.00
Light Blue	$5.00
Dark Blue	$5.00
Yellow	$5.00

Cornflower #2, 4 1/4"

Red	$100.00+
Light Blue	$100.00+
Dark Blue	$100.00+
Yellow	$100.00+

1947 Cornflower ad

This is a nice ad showing the cornflower #2 glasses. It sells for $10.00 and up.

1942 ad, $15.00

1948 Forget-Me-Not

This Swankyswig set came in four colors, red, yellow, dark blue, and light blue, and in two sizes, 3 1/4" and 3 1/2". This is an easy set to put together. Look for ones with labels and lids. There are some that are marked on the bottom with a circle with an L inside for the Libbey Glass Co.®. They are harder to find and will command a premium price.

Label glass, $12.00

Forget-Me-Not, 3 1/4"

Red	$4.00
Light Blue	$4.00
Dark Blue	$4.00
Yellow	$4.00

Forget-Me-Not, 3 1/2"

Red	$4.00
Light Blue	$4.00
Dark Blue	$4.00
Yellow	$4.00

19

This glass can also be found in a 4 1/2" glass. They are rare and the only color I have seen is Dark Blue.

Forget-Me-Not, 4 1/2"

Red	rare
Light Blue	rare
Dark Blue	rare
Yellow	rare

1950 Forget-Me-Not Ad
This is a nice ad showing the Forget-Me-Not glasses.

1950 ad, $12.00

1950 Tulip #3

This set came in four colors, red, green, yellow, and light blue, and in three sizes, 3 1/4", 3 7/8", and 4 3/4". Note that there are some glasses that are missing their leaf; these may have been factory rejects. For a short time in 1951 these were also produced with just the molded ring and no flower design.

Light Blue

Dark Blue

Red

Yellow

Tulip #3, 3 1/4"

Red	$4.00
Yellow	$4.00
Light Blue	$4.00
Dark Blue	$4.00

Tulip #3, 3 7/8"

Red	$4.00
Yellow	$4.00
Light Blue	$4.00
Dark Blue	$4.00

Tulip #3, 4 3/4"

Red	$35.00
Yellow	$35.00
Light blue	$35.00
Dark blue	$35.00

1951 Crystal Petal

This glass was produced for only a short time. It's a plain glass with 24 molded flutes on the bottom. It came in only one size, 3 3/4". These are a little hard to find due to a short production run, but I found one for 50 cents for this book, so don't pay a high price. This could change; we'll have to wait and see.

Full Crystal Petal glass, rare

Crystal Petal glass, $1.00

1951 Petal Ad
Here is a nice ad shows the Petal glass.

1951 Crystal Petal ad, $7.00

1953 Bustlin' Betsy

This set of glasses came in red, green, yellow, orange, brown, and blue, and in three sizes: 3 1/4", 3 3/4", and 4 3/4". This is an easy set if you're only collecting the 3 1/4" or 3 3/4", but if you are looking for the 4 3/4" they can be more expensive to obtain. There has also been a Bustlin' Betsy reported in burgundy.

Red, Blue, Green

Brown, Orange, Yellow

Bustlin' Betsy, 3 1/4"			Bustlin' Betsy, 4 3/4"		
	Red	$4.00		Red	$25.00 to $40.00
	Green	$4.00		Green	$25.00 to $40.00
	Blue	$4.00		Blue	$25.00 to $40.00
	Yellow	$4.00		Yellow	$25.00 to $40.00
	Orange	$4.00		Orange	$25.00 to $40.00
	Brown	$4.00		Brown	$25.00 to $40.00
Bustlin' Betsy, 3 3/4"					
	Red	$4.00			
	Green	$4.00			
	Blue	$4.00			
	Yellow	$4.00			
	Orange	$4.00			
	Brown	$4.00			

1953 Bustlin' Betsy Box Ad

This was a mail in premium off of a cheese box for a cheese cutter and also shows the Bustlin' Betsy glasses. It sells any ware from $10.00 up to $30.00 depending on condition. This is from *Lane Howell's collection.*

1954 Antique #1

This set came in six colors red, green, black, orange, brown, and blue, and three sizes: 3 1/4", 3 3/4 " and 4 3/4". **Don't confuse the 4 3/4" with the 4 5/8" 1974 Canadian series.** The 4 3/4" glasses are hard to find and are increasing in price. They have sold for as high as $77.00 each.

Label glass, $12.00

Antique #1, 3 1/4"

Red	$4.00
Green	$4.00
Blue	$4.00
Black	$4.00
Orange	$4.00
Brown	$4.00

Antique #1, 3 3/4"

Red	$4.00
Green	$4.00
Blue	$4.00
Black	$4.00
Orange	$4.00
Brown	$4.00

Antique #1, 4 3/4"

Red	$40.00++
Green	$40.00++
Blue	$40.00++
Black	$40.00++
Orange	$40.00++
Brown	$40.00++

1955 Bachelor Button

This set came with red and white flowers and green leaves and also in red and white flowers with no leaves and in three sizes 3 1/4", 3 3/4" and 4 3/4".

Bachelor Button, 3 1/4"
             Red/white/green $5.00
             Red/white $10.00
Bachelor Button, 3 3/4"
             Red/white/green $3.00
             Red/white $8.00

Bachelor Button, 4 3/4"
             Red/white/green $10.00
             Red/white   unknown

Bachelor Buttons with Labels

This photo shows the various labels that can be found on the Bachelor button glasses. They sell for $22.00 and up.

Label glasses, $25.00+ each

1956 Kiddie Cup

This set of Swankyswigs came in red, green, yellow, orange, brown, and blue, and in 3 1/4", 3 3/4" and 4 3/4" sizes. There is even a shot glass with the green Kiddie Cup Cat and Rabbit; what a rare find for one of our Swankyswig collector. Someone did this at the glass factory and it is not a cheese glass but sure would make a great addition to any one's collection. The Kiddie Cup glass is the most recognized cheese glass to collectors and to non-collectors. Note: This was spelled Cup not Kup, see boxes.

Kiddie Cup, 3 1/4"

Red	$5.00
Green	$5.00
Blue	$5.00
Black	$5.00
Orange	$5.00
Brown	$5.00

Kiddie Cup, 3 3/4"

Red	$5.00
Green	$5.00
Blue	$5.00
Black	$5.00
Orange	$5.00
Brown	$5.00

Kiddie Cup, 4 3/4"

Red	$30.00 and up
Green	$30.00 and up
Blue	$30.00 and up
Black	$30.00 and up
Orange	$30.00 and up
Brown	$30.00 and up

1960 Hostess Design

This Swankyswig has a fluted design with a square base and came in 5 sizes, 3 1/2", 3 1/4", 3 3/4", 4 5/8", and 5 5/8"

With label, $10.00

3 1/8", 3 1/4", 3 3/4", 4 5/8", 5 5/8", $1.00 each

1960 Ad

This is a nice ad from 1960 showing the Hostess Design.

So many foods taste better when you Cheez Whiz 'em

You don't even need a recipe to make wonderful cheese dishes with Kraft's amazing pasteurized process cheese spread, Cheez Whiz. Just spoon its golden goodness into hot split baked potatoes and you have some-thing *special*. Heat Cheez Whiz (over low heat) and it *becomes* a satin-smooth cheese sauce for vegetables, fish, pasta. Or, right from the jar, spread Cheez Whiz for snacks and sandwiches.

Seven flavors for quick snacks and sandwiches

There's always something good for snacking when your refrigerator holds several glasses of Kraft's flavory pasteurized process cheese spreads. Children particularly like Kraft Pimento, Olive-Pimento, Pineapple and Bacon spreads. More sophisticated flavors are Old English Brand, Smokelle and Kraft Roka Blue. Never let yourself be without sev-eral of these handy Kraft favorites.

Hostess ad, $5.00

1968 Coin Design

This glass has thumb-sized indents around the base. It came in three sizes and was also used for the 1975 Bicentennial glass.

Full glass, $25.00

Coin, 3 1/8", 3 1/4", 3 3/4", $1.00 each

From Lane's Collection (5Texas5)

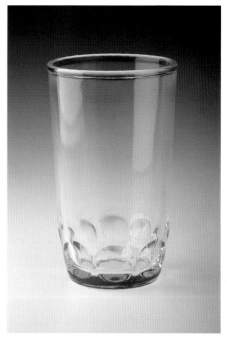

1975 Tulip Bicentennial

These Swankyswigs came in red, green, and yellow, and in only one size, 3 3/4". They were made for a short time in 1975, but due to the high cost of screen painting they were limited in number. They have a thumb-print pattern going around the base and seem to be found more on the west coast.

Red, $15.00; Green, $20.00; Yellow, $15.00

Store Display
Here is a store display showing the Tulip Bicentennial glasses. Rare

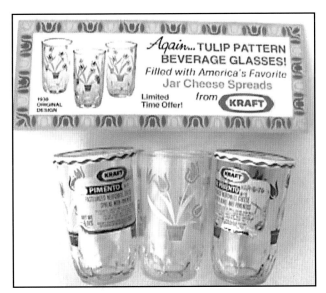

In-store display ad, rare. Glass with label, $25.00

1976 Colonial

This Swankyswig is clear glass with a waffle-diamond pattern in the center of the glass and a banded diamond pattern on the bottom. It came in two sizes; 3 3/4" and 4 3/8".

1976 Colonial, 3 3/4", 4 3/8",
$1.00 each

1978 and 1983 Petal Star

This glass was produced in 1978 with just the petal star and again in 1983 with the Petal Star and the words 1933-1983 50th Anniversary.

1978 Petal, $0.50; w/label, $3.00. 1983 petal, $0.50; w/label, $3.00

Petal Star, 3 3/4"

1978   Petal
1983   50th

Special-Issue Glasses

These Special Issue glasses are among the hardest to locate of any glasses that Kraft used to promote their cheese spread. The World War II glass with a label is a rare find for anyone. The Wheeling Centennial glass can be found with a little looking.

But when you find any of the other glasses shown on the following pages, you will have a rare glass to show with your collection. Most of these were given out at different events from the 1930s to the 1940s. There are other glasses that aren't illustrated, like the special glass with the Kraft Del Monte red tulip #1, and other glasses not yet known. So keep on looking and let us know when you find any rare glass.

1936 Texas Centennial

The Texas Centennial Swankyswig was distributed only in the state of Texas in honor of its 100th Anniversary. The black and blue glasses are fairly easy to obtain and sell for less than the red or green glasses. You can also find this in a 4 7/8" inch cobalt blue glass with white lettering.

Black, $14.00   Cobalt, $40.00

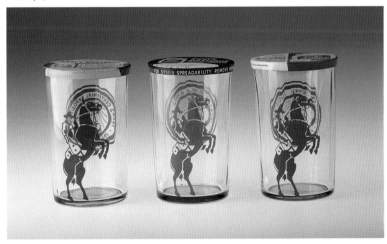

Blue, $14.00; Green, $22.00; Red, $22.00

1936 Wheeling Centennial

I'm including this glass because it is listed in a popular Depression glass book but I haven't yet confirmed that it is a Swankyswig. The glass is 4 7/8" high. Anyone who has any more information on it please let me know

1936, $28.00

1937 Kraft® Convention

Here is a nice glass it is 4 3/4" high. It has the following words on the glass, "Kraft Sales Convention Palace Hotel Jan 23-24, 1937; San Francisco California." On the back it reads "San Francisco – Oakland, Bay Bridge Nov. 12, 1936." This celebrated the opening of the San Francisco-Oakland Bay Bridge in 1936 and the Golden Gate Bridge in 1937. I only have seen two of this Swankyswig on the Internet auctions. Rare

Rare

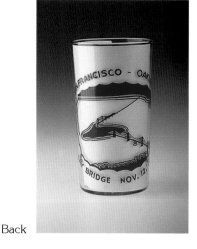

Back

World War II Glasses

This is an undecorated glass used during the war. It was a popular item for families to ship to servicemen overseas. They can be found in Europe and also in the USA. I haven't seen any with a label for sale on the internet or at the antique markets. You can find them with all of the available labels of the time with some searching. Should sell for $15.00 and up. This glass is from *Lane Howell's* collection.

Plain glass, $1.00; w/label, $20.00

1941 Del Monte

This is a wonderful glass. It is the Cornflower #1 glass from the Posy series and has the following words on the glass, "Greetings From Kraft, California Retail, Association, Grocers and Merchants, Del Monte, Sept. 1941." The back has the cornflower from the Posy pattern.

This glass is from *Joyce Jackson* collection and is rare. There is also one with the Tulip #2 pattern.

Rare, this one sold for $425.00

Back

1947 Chehalis Washington

This was an Opening Day Souvenir glass that was handed out by Kraft Foods Company at the September 13,1947 Lewis-Pacific Dairymen's Association in Chehalis, Washington. It is a 3 1/2" glass and can be found in red and blue. This glass is from *Lane Howell's* collection.

Red or green, $150.00 to $200.00

1948 4-H Club

I know that there are at less 13 of these glasses. I bought 9 out of a 4-H collection. They measure 3 1/2" high and were only produced in green. They were handed out to the guests of J.L. Kraft at the farewell luncheon on December 2, 1948.

Rare, $320.00

34

1949 Santa Barbara

What a wonderful glass. "Greetings on your Golden Anniversary, from us at Kraft®, California retail Grocers & Merchants Association, Santa Barbara, 1949." This glass is 3 1/2" high and is rare. This glass is from *Lane Howell's* collection.

Rare

Mail-in Premium Leaf Plate

This Swankyswig plate *is not glass*. It is the leaf-shape saucer/snack plate made by HLC as a premium for Kraft. It is model number 1082 in the HLC modeling logbook, first made in March of 1938. They were available in two colors, Fiesta red or green. The advertising lid reads, "This Smart Snack Plate for only 25¢ and two jar labels from Kraft Cheese Spreads" / "Fiesta" Colors; Red or Green," / "Snack Plate made by the makers of 'Fiesta' Ware." They sell for $100.00+. Sorry I couldn't find a photo for this plate.

2003 Kraft Food 100th Anniversary

2003 Kraft Food 100th Anniversary glasses.

Look-Alikes

You will find other companies used the same blanks for their glasses. The most popular ones are the Rooster and the Cherry glasses. They are hard to find so even if you don't want to include them in your collection, buy them anyway to sell or trade to others

Cherries

Cherries are 3 1/2" glasses and came in five colors, with Blue and Gold bringing the highest price.

Cherries, 3 1/2"

Maroon	$20.00+
Gold	$35.00+
Green	$20.00+
Black	$20.00+
Blue	$35.00+

The Roosters and Forget-Me-Not

The Roosters is a well sought after look-alike glass and sells for $20.00 and up. The black over red has sold for as high as $56.00. The Forget-Me-Not glass at the top is what I think to be a Swankyswig. It is on the same blank as the Posy series glasses and the paint color also matches, but no other one like it or in other colors has been reported.

Rooster

Red with Blue lines	$20.00
Red with Black lines	$20.00
Blue with Red lines	$20.00
Red with Blue lines	$20.00
Black with Red lines	$25.00
Red and Blue Forget-Me-Not	$20.00

1930s Band

There are a lot of glasses with different bands on them. This is just a short list. I would say a lot of them could be from Shefford® Cheese Co. or Swift® Co.

The first glass is 3 1/2" high and has two pin stripes, red then blue, and a bigger band in red.

This next glass is 3 1/2" glass with a blue band then a yellow band.

Blue-Yellow
bands, $20.00

Red-Blue-Red
bands, $20.00

1943 Shefford Glass

This is a Shefford® cheese glass and has two gold bands around the top. Libbey® made this glass. The ad is from 1943.

1943 ad,
$5.00

Gold Band, $2.00;
with label, $25.00

Canadian Only Issue
1936 Galleon

This is a hard set of Canadian glasses to finish There is only one size 3 1/4" and there are five colors. Some of these have sold for $70.00 and more in Internet auctions. These prices are for mint glasses only.

Galleon, 3 1/4"

Red	$22.00+
Blue	$22.00+
Black	$40.00+
Yellow	$45.00+
Green	$40.00+

1971 Star #2

This is the easiest glass to find in the Canadian series. It comes in only one color, orange, and one size, 4 3/4". You can even find labeled glasses without any trouble.

Lid, $3.00

Star, $4.00; w/label, $8.00

1974 Wildlife

This is a hard set to complete. The glasses are 4 5/8" high and come in one color, Black. The Bear is scarce and has sold for the highest price so far. Next in rarity would be the Goose, and the easiest to find are the Red Fox and Moose, though they still will bring a nice price.

Red Fox, $22.00+

Goose, $24.00+

Bear, $50.00+

Moose, $24.00+

1974 Ethnic

The Ethnic set is a hard one too finish. They measure 4 5/8" high. The Blue Mexico glass seems to be the hardest one to find, followed by the Yellow Calypso.

Mexico $45.00

Maroon, Scotland $9.00

Red, India $9.00

Ethnic, 4 5/8"

Red India	$9.00
Light Green Calypso	$40.00
Maroon Scotland	$9.00
Yellow Scotland	$25.00
Blue Mexico	$45.00

1974 Antique #2

This set is different from the Antique #1. The Antique #2 glasses have the same pattern on each glass and come in five different colors. They measure 4 5/8" high. The Antique #1 glasses a different pattern on each glass, come in six different colors, and are 4 3/4" high. This set is still hard to find in Lime Green, Orange, and Black.

Red, Blue, Lime Green

Antique #2, 4 5/8"

Red	$9.00
Lime Green	$17.00
Orange	$22.00
Black	$32.00
Blue	$9.00

1975 Sports

The Sport series has five different glasses in its set, each measuring 4 5/8" high. The Hockey glass is the most sought after glass to collectors. Some collectors doubt that it even exists. The Soccer glass would be the second hardest to find.

Football, Red, $9.00; Baseball, Red, $9.00; Skiing, Blue, $9.00;
Soccer, Dark Green, $40.00; Hockey, N/A

Canadian Look-Alikes

These are nice glasses to add to you collection. There are three that I know of, Grape, Cherry and Pineapple, but there could be more.

Pineapple, $4.00; Cherry, $4.00; Grape, $4.00

Australian Only Issue

There are many different decorated glasses that Kraft used for their cheese spread in Australia. The most sought after glasses are the Disneyland and Pinocchio series. With all the Disney and Pinocchio collectors buying them to go with their collections and Swankyswig collectors trying to get them, too, the prices just keep on going up and up.

Our information is still limited on these glasses. Let us know if you can provide any additional information.

This is a close up of a 1949 ad showing Australian Wildflower glasses.

A nice 1949 Australian ad showing Wildflower glasses, $25.00+

1935 Band

Information on this glass is limited. The Band glass is 3 5/16" high and has a red band on top with a black band below. There are two different varieties on the band placement: one has the bands 1/8" apart and the other has the bands 3/16" apart. Sorry we have no photo for this one

This little box isn't a glass but it does look nice with our collection of Australian glasses. It sold for $14.00.

1935 Playing Cards

The Playing Cards Swankyswigs came in two sizes, 3 3/8" and 4 3/4". They came in four patterns Diamonds-Red, Hearts-Red, Clubs-Black, and Spades-Black with the pattern repeated 4 times around the glass. Watch out for the look-alike glasses. One is 4 3/4" high with the suit repeated 8 times. The other look-a-like glass is 4 3/8" high and has the suits near the top.

Playing Cards, 3 3/8"

Clubs	$25.00
Spades	$25.00
Diamonds	$25.00
Hearts	$25.00

Playing Cards, 4 3/4"

Clubs	N/A
Spades	N/A
Diamonds	N/A
Hearts	N/A

1935 Ad
This ad sells for $25.00 to $35.00.

1940 Pinocchio

The Pinocchio series came in two different sizes, 3 1/4" and 4 3/4" high. This is a hard set of Swankyswigs to finish with all the different colors. They also have a little saying on the back of each. Prices are getting higher on these; expect to pay anywhere from $30.00 and up. Jiminy Cricket has sold for as high as $56.00 and I haven't seen any of the large glasses for sale. These glasses are form the *Carol Nelson collection.*

Cleo, Red or Blue, $35.00+

Figaro, Black, $35.00+   Stromboli, Black, $35.00+

Fairy, Blue, $40.00+

Jiminy Cricket, Light Green, Dark Green, Red, or Blue, $40.00 to $65.00+

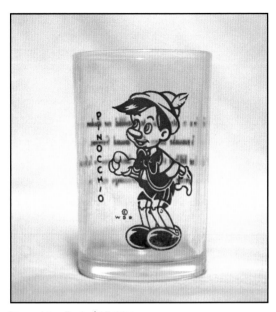

Pinocchio, Red, $35.00+

Geppetto, Black or Brown, $35.00+

1940-41 Disneyland

The Disneyland Swankyswigs came in only one size, 3 1/4", and had Huey, Dewey, & Louie on the same glass, and came in two colors, Light Green and Dark Green. The other glasses in the series featured Donald Duck in Dark Blue and Light Blue, Mickey in Black, and Minnie in Red. Mickey and Minnie have sold for $105.00 for the pair, and they are getting harder to find. These glasses are form the *Carol Nelson collection.*

Donald Duck, Dark Blue or Light Blue, $40.00+

Dewey, Huey, & Louie, Light Green or Dark Green, $50.00+

Mickey Mouse, Black $65.00+

Minnie Mouse, Red $40.00+

1948 Tulip #1

The Tulip #1 came in three sizes, 3 1/4", 3 5/8", and 4 3/4". The 4 3/4" came in dark green and yellow and have Tulips repeated 4 time around the glass. The 3 5/8" came in Light blue, dark green and red and also had 4 Tulips repeated around the glass. .The 3 1/4" came in light blue, dark blue, light green, orange, red, white, light yellow, and yellow and had only 3 Tulips repeated around the glass. These glasses are from *Joyce Jackson's "jjpick"* Collection.

Tulip #1, 3 1/4"

Light Blue	$8.00
Blue	$8.00
Light green	$8.00
Green	$8.00
Light Orange	$8.00
Orange	$8.00
Red	$8.00
White	$8.00
Light Yellow	$8.00
Yellow	$8.00

Tulip #1, 3 5/8"

Light Blue	$8.00
Green	$8.00
Red	$8.00

Tulip #1, 4 3/4"

Dark Green	N/A
Yellow	N/A

1951-52, 1954 Tulip #2

The Tulip #2 Swankyswigs came in only one size, 3 5/8", with four embossed rings around the top of the glasses. They came in the following colors, Light Blue, Dark Blue, Light Green, Orange, Red, White, and Yellow. This Swankyswig was reissued in 1954.

Tulip #2, 3 5/8"

Light Blue	$8.00
Dark Blue	$8.00
Light Green	$8.00
Orange	$8.00
Red	$8.00
White	$8.00
Yellow	$8.00

1949-50 Wildflower

The Wildflower Swankyswigs came in one size, 3 3/8", with nine different flower patterns. The flower was repeated four times around the glass and the name of the flower was printed near the bottom. These glasses are from *Joyce Jackson's "jjpick"* Collection.

Wildflower, 3 3/8"

Blue Bell	$9.00
Blue Flax Lily	$9.00
Bottle Brush	$9.00
Flannel Flower	$9.00
Maiden Hair Fern	$9.00
Wattle	$9.00
Xmas Bells	$9.00
Xmas Bush	$9.00
Spider Flower, Dark Green or White	$9.00

Blue Bell, $9.00

Xmas Bells, $9.00

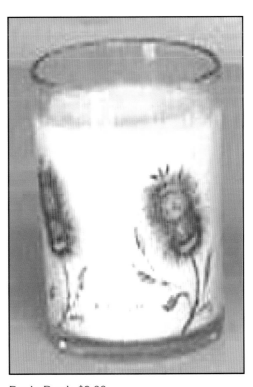

Bottle Brush $9.00

1949 Wildflower Ad
This ad sells for $25.00 and up

Close-up of the Wildflower ad.

56

1950-51 Star

The Star Swankyswig set came in two sizes, 3 3/8" and 4 3/4" high. The 4 3/4" glasses came in five colors: Red, Light Blue, Dark Blue, Light Green, and Dark Green. The 3 3/8" glass came in Red, Orange, White, Yellow, and Dark Blue.

Star glasses, $10.00+ each

Star, 3 3/8"

Red	$9.00
Orange	$9.00
White	$9.00
Yellow	$9.00
Dark Blue	$9.00

1953 Flannel Flowers

The Flannel Flower Swankyswigs come in eleven colors and only one size, 3 3/4" high. They have four rings embossed around the top of the glass.

Flannel Flowers, 3 3/4"

Red	$9.00
Light Red	$9.00
Green	$9.00
Light Green	$9.00
Blue	$9.00
Light Blue	$9.00
Yellow	$9.00
Light Yellow	$9.00
Orange	$9.00
Light Orange	$9.00
White	$9.00

Australian Look-Alikes

I see these glasses being sold as Swankyswigs, but they are not Kraft® glasses. The first glass is a Koala bear. The second glass is the teddy bear party, the third glass is wildflower, and the last glass is Monkey Circus; it comes in four colors.

$4.00 each

Other Items
Boxes

If you want a challenge this would be the hardest thing to collect. Lane has sent me photos of his collection of boxes. Note that the one box has Snow White and the Seven Dwarfs on it. We still don't have a glass to show for this. These boxes are from *Lane Howell's* collection.

Snow White, $50.00

Plain, $20.00

Cream Spread Cheese, $20.00

Band, $50.00

Circle and Dot, $50.00+

Bachelor Buttons, $45.00+

Bustlin' Betsy, $45.00+

Kiddie Cup, $45.00+

Lids

This will be an interesting challenge to collect. Lids come with all kinds of advertising on them. Note that one has the Star glass on it, one has the Canadian Galleon glass, and there is also one showing the Tulip #1 Swankyswig. The first lid used was the K with the words: "This is a thin drinking glass, to open first puncture – tap around top edge." Prices are for mint lids. These lids are out of *Lane Howell's* and our collections.

Galleon, $50.00

Star, $50.00

Bing, $40.00

Bing, $40.00

Gildersleeve, $40.00

Gildersleeve, $40.00

Kraft® Loaf Cheese, $20.00

Cap Lifter, $20.00

Kraft® K, $15.00

Caramels Bag, $20.00

Kids, $20.00

Boy, $20.00

Miracle Sandwich Spread, $20.00

Malted Milk, $15.00

Malted Milk, $15.00

Malted Milk, $15.00

Krafttone, $20.00

Old English, $20.00

7 Minutes, $20.00

9 Minutes, $30.00

Ration Points, $20.00

Mayonnaise, $15.00

Mustards, $10.00

Mustards, $10.00

Mustards, $8.00

Mustards, $8.00

Mustards, $10.00

Mustards, $8.00

French Dressing, $20.00

French Dressing, $20.00

French Dressing, $20.00

Large mayo lid, $20.00

Miracle Whip, $10.00

Mayonnaise, $15.00

Velveeta, $25.00

Philadelphia Cream Cheese, $15.00

Parkay, $15.00

Snacks, $20.00

Cheeses, $15.00

Collect, $20.00

Cheese Spread, $20.00

This product replaces KRAFT Roquefort Cream Cheese Spread

Roquefort, $30.00

Important!, $30.00

Cheese Spread, $7.00

Australian, $9.00

1970s Canada, $3.00

Labels

Adding labeled glasses can make your collection more interesting. Glasses shown on the next couple of pages are only a few different possibilities you may find. Check out the display rack in Lane's collection. Most of these glasses are from *Lane Howell's* and our collection.

There are eight different labels used from 1933 to 1939: Pineapple, Kay, Teez, Olive Pimentos, Limburger, Pimentos, Roquefort, and Old English. In 1941 Roka was added, and in 1951 they added Cheese and Bacon. Prices are for MINT Labels.

Display rack, $100.00

Ring, $100.00

Circle-Dot, $50.00

Tulip, $50.00

Tulip, $50.00

Star, $50.00

Carnival, $50.00

Forget-Me-Not, $20.00

Forget-Me-Not, $20.00

79

Forget-Me-Not, 3 1/4", $20.00; 3 1/2", $20.00. From the *Carol Nelson collection*.

Posy Cornflower #1: 3 1/2", $20.00; 3 1/4", $20.00. From the *Carol Nelson collection*.

Antique #1, $20.00

Antique #1, $20.00

Kiddie Cup, 4 3/4", $40.00. From the *Carol Nelson collection*.

Antique #2, never opened, $100.00.
From the *Carol Nelson collection*.

Star #2, $8.00

Kiddie Cup, $20.00

Sports Series, $20.00+. From the
Carol Nelson collection.

More Advertising & Displays

Advertisements out of vintage popular magazines make a nice addition to your collection. Kraft started advertising in magazines in 1935, which makes a advertisements a very good source for dating the glasses. There are a lot more out there to be found, besides the ones shown here and throughout this book.

This first one is a 1941 Posy ad.

1941 Posy pattern ad, $15.00

1947 Posy
Cornflower #2
ad, $14.00

1949 Forget-Me-Not Ads
   The next ads show the Forget-Me-Not glasses.

1949 Roka ad,
$9.00

1949 Old English ad, $9.00

1949 Old English, $9.00

1950 #2 Tulip ad

This ad shows the Tulip #2 glasses.

1950 Tulip #2 ad, $9.00

Close-up of Tulip #2 ad.

Refrigerator Graphic Showing Swankyswigs

Neat ad with Kraft® Cheese glasses in the refrigerator door. $4.00

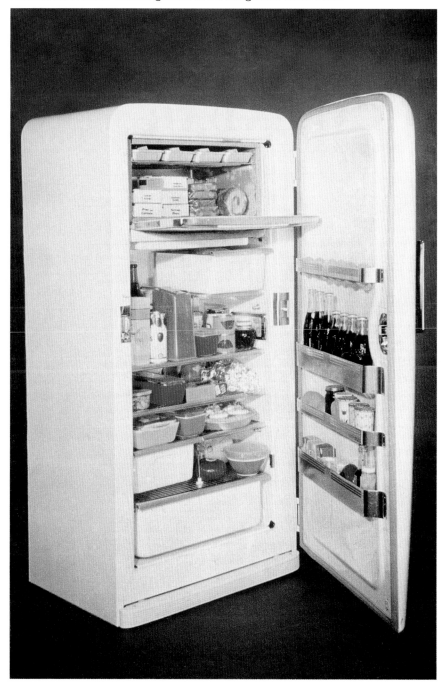

Plain Glasses

1948 Plain glasses,
$4.00

Fiesta Glasses

1941 Fiesta glasses, $4.00

Display Glasses

Here are two glasses that are painted to look like cheese inside.

Display glasses, $100.00+

Cook Books

I just started compiling a list of Kraft cook books with Swankyswigs advertising. There are more out there, so let me know what you find.

1934 Band

Smart Savories from a Century of Progress is dated 1934. This is the first paper advertising that I know of showing the Band glass.

Smart Savories from a Century of Progress cookbook, showing Band glasses, $20.00

Roquefort Cream Crumpets

Kraft Roquefort Cream Spread   Milk
Worcestershire sauce   Fresh bread

● Slightly soften the smooth, zestful Roquefort Cream Spread with milk. Add a dash of Worcestershire sauce. Cut very thin slices from a loaf of fresh white bread. Trim the crusts. Spread each slice with the Roquefort Cream mixture, roll up like a jelly roll and fasten with toothpicks. Toast on all sides under the broiler. Serve the Crumpets hot at tea, or with a luncheon salad. If Kraft Portion Roquefort Cheese is used, add twice the weight of "Philadelphia" Cream Cheese (1½-ounce portion of Kraft Roquefort to 3-ounce package "Philadelphia" Cream Cheese), blend thoroughly, moisten slightly with milk and season with Worcestershire sauce.

KRAFT Swiss

Broiled Open Sandwich

Bread   Broiled bacon
Sliced tomatoes   Kraft Swiss Cheese
          Kraft Kitchen-Fresh Mayonnaise

● Toast a slice of bread (crusts trimmed) on one side. Spread the untoasted side with Kraft Mayonnaise, cover with a thick slice of peeled tomato, then with two strips of partially broiled bacon. Finally, a generous slice of the good, nut-sweet Kraft Swiss Cheese. Toast under a very low broiler flame until the cheese is melted, and serve hot. Here is a quick trick for any bridge party hostess. Remember it for little Sunday night suppers, too—and for late-at-night refreshments.

Band glasses in the *Smart Savories* cookbook.

1930s Star

This *Favorite Recipes* cookbook can be found dated 1936 & 1938. Both show the small Star Swankyswig, but the 1936 one also shows the large Star glass (see the Star section).

Favorite Recipes cookbook, 1936, $15.00; 1938, $8.00

1930s Circle and Dot

The *Appetite Tempters* came in two variations, both with the same cover. One has seven cheese spread varieties and the other has eight. The eight varieties show the Circle and Dot glasses. The other one has plain glasses. I haven't seen any of these cookbooks showing Circle and Dot Swankyswigs for sale.

Appetite Tempters with ad for seven varieties of cheese spreads featuring plain glasses, $4.00

Appetite Tempters cookbook, no date

Appetite Tempters with ad for eight varieties of cheese spreads featuring the Circle and Dot glasses, $25.00

1940s Forget-Me-Not and Cornflower #2

At least two versions of *Appetite Tempters and Sandwiches* were printed with this cover. One has an advertisement illustrated with Forget-Me-Not Swankyswigs. The other has Cornflower #2 Swankyswigs.

1940s

Forget-Me-Not $20.00
Cornflower #2 $20.00

1942 Posy

The Cheese Cook Book is dated 1942 and shows the Posy glasses inside.

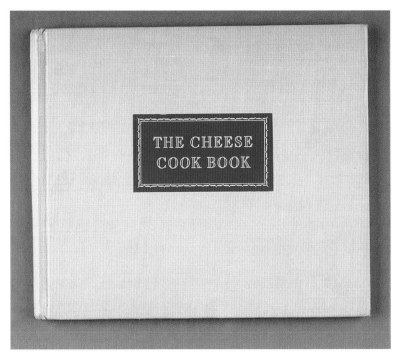

The Cheese Cook Book, 1942, showing the Posy glasses, $9.00

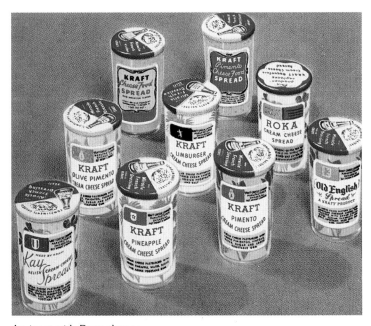

An inset with Posy glasses.

1943 Posy Black and White

Cheese Recipes for Wartime Meals is dated 1943 and shows the Posy glasses in a black and white photo.

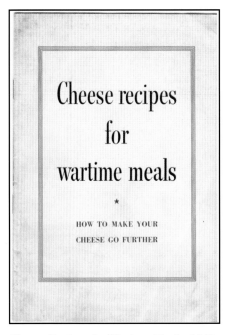

Cheese Recipes for Wartime Meals, 1943, with Posy ad, $9.00

Posy ad from *Cheese Recipes for Wartime Meals*